The Odyssey of the Horny Owl

Dennis Hardcastle: Captain
Sandy Lecklider: First Mate
Marie Mekler: Purser
Barb Eccker: Kedger

The Odyssey of the Horny Owl

Published by Dennis Hardcastle

ISBN: 978-0-615-79974-2
Library of Congress Control Number: 2013906688

Dedicated to the Florida Wildlife Federation

Since 1937, the mission of the non-profit Florida Wildlife Federation has been the conservation of Florida's natural resources so that present and future Florida citizens may continue to live in an outstanding natural environment.

Preface

We live in Sea Oaks, Vero Beach, Florida. Sea Oaks is a community on the barrier island, bounded to the east by the Atlantic Ocean and to the west by the Indian River.

In 1992, we bought a 20' pontoon boat for use on the Indian River. Activities included cocktail cruises, family picnics on the spoil islands and going north for dinner at "Capt. Hirams" or south to "Mr. Manatees."

After a year or so these excursions became somewhat repetitive so we made our first big trip across Florida, coast to coast. We made several of these runs with various crews, but the problem was that many other boats, most of them bigger than The Horny Owl, tended to "over wake" us.

We started traveling outside Florida. We went down the Erie Canal, the Trent Severn Canal, and the Ottawa and Temiskawa rivers in Canada.

Then in 1993, we discovered Central and North Florida in our own backyard. That was a game changer!

Over 100 three day trips have been taken by the permanent crew of three women and one man.

Because we travel without spouses, (one spouse explained, "We don't enjoy watching grass grow,") these trips have been the subject of great speculation by our neighbors in Sea Oaks despite our protestations. Honestly, the name of the boat didn't help!

Finally, we were asked to participate in a series of "Florida Nature" lectures at Sea Oaks on the condition we tell what really happens on these infamous trips.

This book is the result of that "lecture" and is a distillation of thousands of photographs taken by the crew and the ship's logs meticulously kept by the First Mate.

When we started the trips in 1994, the average age of the crew was 65. It is now 83 and we are still tripping. Enjoy!

Table of Contents

Introduction

After discovering Northern Florida, we are constantly amazed at how many hours we can travel on small streams or creeks and how few people and boats are encountered on these trips.

Whenever we set out on a trip, the only destination we have is getting on the water. Once on it, the destination, like the water itself, may move slowly and we just go with it.

Also, in these days of gadgets and gidgets, instant and constant communication and breaking news, we realize how incredibly relaxing and refreshing it is to be on a narrow creek without them…just looking and listening.

Please note this book was not written as a travel guide. In fact, we prefer you don't go to these places! This book is a simple tribute to a very special part of the world with spectacular wildlife and scenery.

Whence the name "The Horny Owl?"

When we bought the boat, we launched it at the Wabasso Boat Ramp and motored around the point of Marsh Island to our home marina at Sea Oaks.

As we came around the point of the island into the Indian River, we saw a great horned owl looking down at us from a low tree branch.

This was obviously a sign from the river gods that this humble pontoon boat should be named "The Great Horned Owl." Even to us, it sounded awfully pretentious.

In a matter of days, with a little help from our friends, it went from "The Great Horned Owl" to "The Horny Owl." This was considerably less pretentious, although at the risk of being considerably more provocative!

(Apologies to our more worldly readers who may have thought the name had been more nobly earned.)

The Great Horned Owl*

"The Horny Owl" at the helm

*The picture of the Great Horned Owl is attributable to ThirdBirdFromTheSun.com, William H. Majoros. It is the only picture not taken by the Crew.

Why a Pontoon Boat?

Just consider
what a boat
has to be for
our kind of trip...

- Comfortable for a
  full day without
  leaving the boat

- Completely open
  so you can easily
  walk from bow to
  stern and side to
  side in order to
  clear obstacles

- Spacious enough
  to carry four
  people and
  equipment

- Big enough to
  sleep four if need
  be

- Easy to run up on shore

- Able to navigate very shallow water

- Easily covered in rain or cold weather

- Reasonably resilient when hitting logs

- High enough to avoid water level threats, i.e. gators

- Low enough to go under low lying bridges and branches

- Light enough to trailer easily

Canoes, kayaks, paddle boards, small hulled boats, and air boats can each meet some of these requirements... but only a pontoon boat can do 'em all!

The

	Marie Mekler	Barb Eccker
Name:	Marie Mekler	Barb Eccker
Title:	Purser	Kedger*
Affinity for Water Activities:	College Swim Team Years of Sailing on Buzzards Bay	Years of Sailing on Lake Michigan & Lake Macatawa
Physical Prowess:	College Champion: Basketball Field Hockey Softball	Only Woman in U.S. to Play on Men's College Tennis Team 1949-1950
Special Duties:	"Keeper of the Money" (trip expenditures) Photographer	"Keeper of the Black Bag" (containing everything from bandaids to power tools) Photographer
Important Physical Attributes:	Doesn't Scare Easily Doesn't Talk Much Good Listener	Doesn't Scare Easily Doesn't Talk Much Good Listener
Family Status:	Great Grandmother	Grandmother

*Kedger: When aground, person who throws anchor and pulls boat, called "Kedging"

Crew

Sandy Lecklider

First Mate

Sailing Alone Since Age 10
World Champion:
Water Ski Jumping 1953
Water Ski Hall of Fame

Bronze Medal in
Senior World Games
Tennis

"Keeper of the Ship's Log"
(every trip documented)
Makes all Travel Arrangements
Back-up Pilot

Doesn't Scare Easily
Doesn't Talk Much
Good Listener

Grandmother

Dennis Hardcastle

Captain

From a Maritime Nation

3rd Place
Egg & Spoon Race
London, 1936

"Keeper of the Grill"
i.e. The Cook

Appropriately Cautious
Doesn't Talk Much
Can't Hear Much

Great Grandfather

Where Do We Go?

The primary rivers we travel on include the Suwannee, St. John's, Oklawaha, Santa Fe and St. Mary's. But most often we find ourselves on the smaller creeks and streams that flow from these main waterways.

It was only while putting this tome together that we realized the wilderness we enjoyed most was the Ocala National Forest situated between the Oklawaha and St. John's rivers.

Discovering the Wilderness of Florida

What's a wilderness? We like the definition that is posted at Juniper Springs State Park near Lake George:

Ask 100 people to define wilderness and you will get 100 different answers. Wilderness is as much an idea as it is a place. It has even been called "a dark and dismal place where wild beasts and birds roam about uncooked." Wilderness is a place "where the earth and community of life are untrammeled by humans," where natural processes operate freely, and human imprint is not evident.

Florida has beautifully kept state parks with most of them in the Northern part of the state. Interestingly the SM (trademark) of the Florida State Park Service is "The Real Florida."

Florida is basically two separate areas, North and South, and they are very different from one another. Central Florida spans both.

The South is subtropical and the North is a temperate climate with more diverse scenery.

The people are also different as are the economies. There have been serious political attempts to separate them on the basis that North Florida has more in common with Georgia, and economically, South Florida would be better off. Just an item of interest. Either way, we'll still keep going!

Typical Waterways and Sights

Merriam Webster Dictionary defines "typical" as "constituting or having the nature of a type."

In the case of the rivers, creeks and streams on which we travel, they are narrow, mostly back water, lush, quiet and beautiful. In this case, "typical" means "constituting or having the type of a nature."

The crew has taken over 5,000 photographs in the last 20 years. These are just a few.

Preparing to launch at Old Town on the Suwannee River. (native: Echo River)

Most of the streams are "black water." The sources of the water are from springs and/or run-off. The run-off from decaying vegetation contains tannic acid, which makes the water a coffee color.

Salt Creek

On Owl Creek trying to find Alexander Springs while looking for submerged logs.

Harris Creek

Haw Creek

Just getting along on Dunn's Creek.

Norris Dead Creek

Norris Dead Creek

Entrance to "Highland Park Fish Camp Marina." (off Norris Dead Creek)

Approaching the Fish Camp.

24

Stopping for lunch, Davenport Landing...amazing that this spot on the narrow, winding Oklawaha River was a passenger steam boat stop in the 19th century.

Oklawaha River (native meaning: Muddy River)

Wekiva River (native meaning: Spring of Water)

Wekiva River

A misty morning start on the Silver River.

Sunset on the St John's River, which is the longest river in Florida. It flows north for over 300 miles.

Springs

It is estimated there are over 700 fresh water springs in Florida.

Some are small, and others are of the first magnitude discharging millions of gallons each day.

The Florida Park Service maintains state parks at some of the bigger springs. They are beautifully kept, and we enjoy visiting them on our trips.

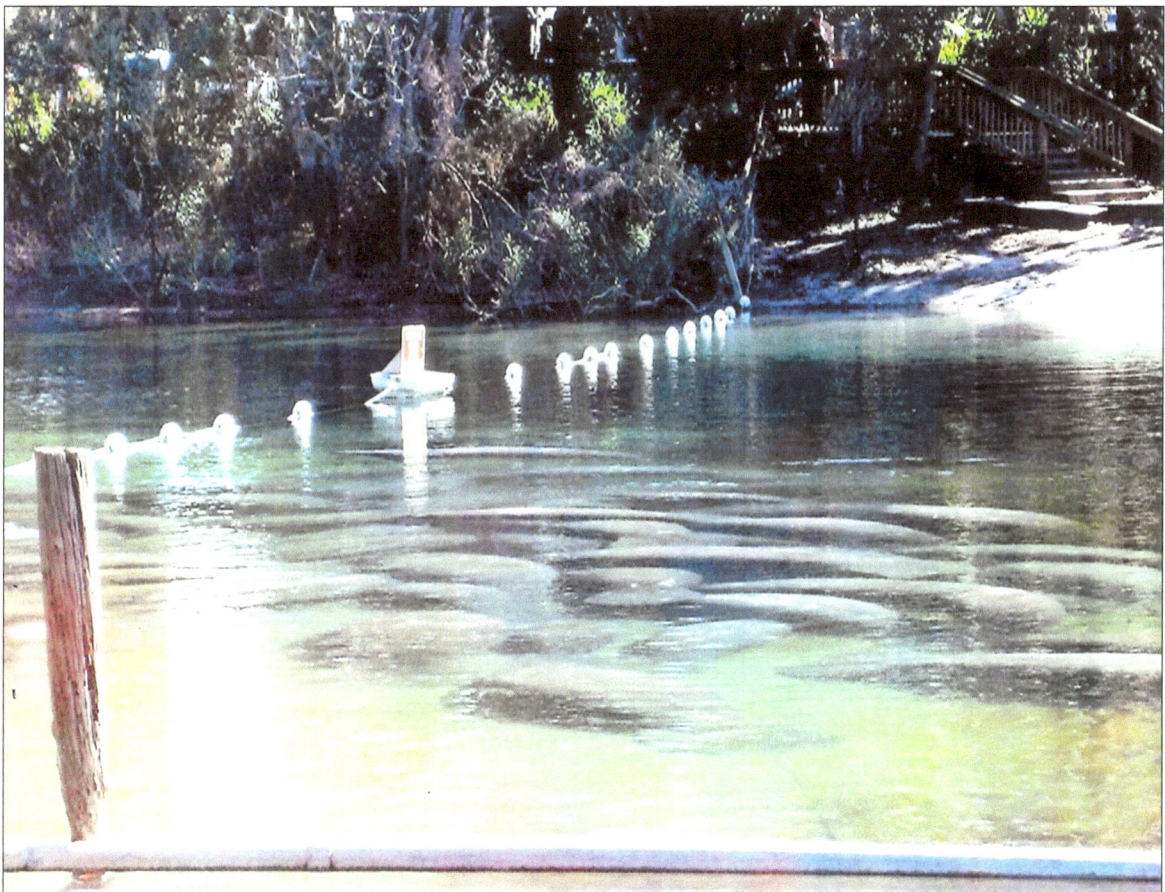

Blue Springs...it was a cold day so manatees were there to keep warm.

Silver River...approaching Silver Springs.

We especially enjoy coming across small springs in less traveled areas.

The springs maintain a constant temperature of around 70 degrees. Contrary to our initial assumption, the springs are not geothermal but simply represent the fact that underground water stays around 70 degrees in Florida.

In addition to rainfall, the springs are a source of water for the surrounding rivers and streams, and are a major underground supply of drinking water as well.

Coming into Ginnie Springs.

Ginnie Springs

Ichetucknee River (native meaning: Beaver Water)

Off of the Ichetucknee River.

Hart Springs...off the Suwannee River, which has many springs.

We don't know if this spring has a name. It was also off the Suwannee River.

Alligators

There are a million or so alligators in Florida. We haven't seen that many but there hasn't been a trip when we haven't seen any. The low water, that unfortunately seems to be prevailing, makes them even more visible.

Oklawaha River...looks old...alligators have been known to live over 70 yrs.

The muscles that close their jaws are very strong. The muscles that open their jaws are relatively weak. One person can hold their jaws shut, they say. We have never tried it and don't intend to!

Little Juniper Creek

A group of alligators is called a "congregation." A group of chickens is called a "flock." A group of churchgoers has a choice.

The Wekiva River was low when we met this congregation.

These look like competing entries in a sculpture exhibition.

Alligators build compost nests. The sex of the newborn is determined by how warm the nest is at the time of incubation. Mid 80 degrees or lower produces females and over 90 degrees produces males.

Eventually however…

…everybody is someone else's lunch in nature.

Brand new alligators on Little Juniper Creek.

A group of vultures enjoying an alligator on Deep Creek.

Gators often have a smile as if thinking about an old joke, like the one that goes "an alligator, a chicken and a pig went into a bar…"

Turtles

You don't hear much about them, yet upwards of 10% of the world's known species of turtles are here in Florida. They've been around for well over 100 million years, but are now in decline.

Ichetucknee River

Santa Fe River...for every alligator we see, we must see 100 turtles.

Manatees

Manatees are gentle, intelligent, 1000 lb. creatures that spend most of their time sleeping underwater, coming up for air every 15 or 20 minutes. Approximately 5000 live in Florida and they, like so many other Florida species, need help to survive.

Manatees used to migrate further south than Florida. Now, in addition to springs, they stay in the warm water produced by power plants along Florida's coast.

Blue Springs

They are herbivores eating plants like mangrove leaves and algae. They eat a lot, up to 10% of their weight each day. Their principal enemies are humans, and human impact on their natural environment. Over the years, hundreds have been killed or mortally wounded by boat propellers.

Their nearest living relative is the elephant. Not surprising!

Birds

Sandhill cranes. The males and females look alike. They can soar above for hours with their six or seven foot wing spans.

East Lake

Ibises rehearsing their Christmas tree pageant. By the way, we learned not to eat lunch under a tree full of ibises!

Ibises huddling for warmth on a cold morning.

Wood storks forage for food, usually frogs, fish and insects. It catches fish by opening its bill under water until a fish swims in. How cool is that!

Old Kissimee River

We think this is a great egret. Egrets have beautiful plumes and were almost wiped out a hundred years ago as their feathers were in demand as hat adornments in the early 20th century.

Salt Spring Run

44

Salivating pelicans perched on a fish pound on St John's River.

This pelican escorted us quite a way on the St. John's River.

Salt Springs Run

Turkey Creek

Saw this blue heron standing on the side of an abandoned canoe. Named him "Claude." As we left, he lost his balance, so we changed his named to "Clumsy Claude."

And, if this isn't an official "night heron"...it should be.

Lake Woodruff

The moorhen is very common throughout the world. They stay close to the edge of swamps. Sometimes referred to as "swamp chickens."

Trout Creek

Our favorite. The limpkin. "Watch bird" of the forest. We passed under the branch and she (or he) gave the loudest yell we've ever heard from a bird.

Flowers

Juniper Creek...river iris.

St. Lucie River...white bushy astor.

Salt Creek...St. John's wort.

Snake Creek... common beggar ticks.

Okeechobee River...spatter dock.

Kissimee River...cactus flower.

Santa Fe River...yellow buttons.

Harry's Creek...swamp lily.

Reflections
Which of these pictures is the reflection?

Water reflections are special gifts we've learned to look for.

We did not see any reflections for many years because even our three mph boat speed created ripples that prevented them from forming.

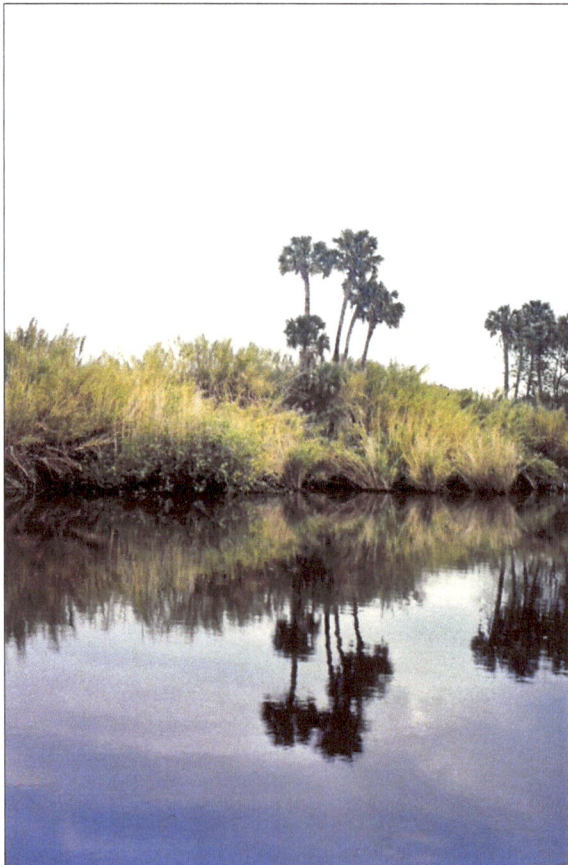

Waterway at Okeechobee
(native meaning: Big Water)

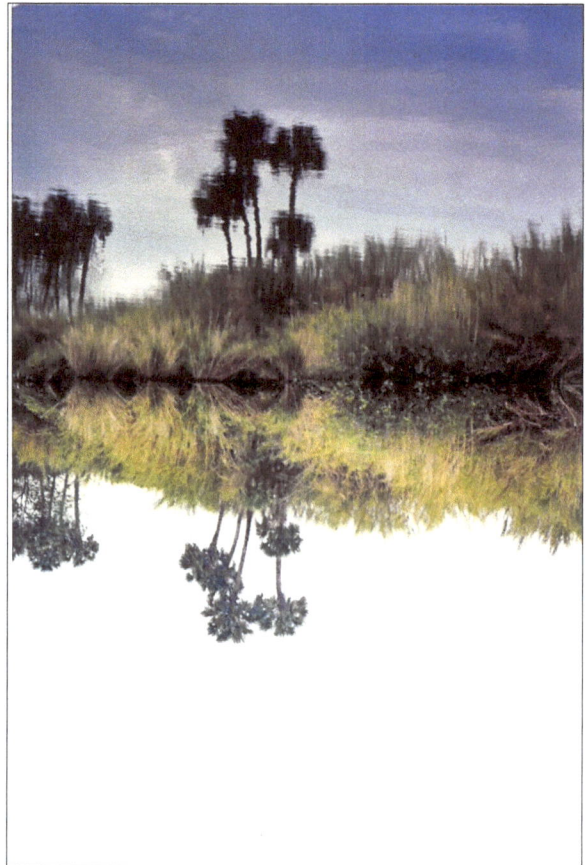

Now, most of the reflections we see occur after we've pulled up for lunch on a side cut and the water has become still.

After a while, these reflections can be almost hypnotic. They are very special.

Up or Down?

Dunn's Creek

Up or Down?

EPA Creek

Up or Down?

Entrance to Buckman Lock.

Up or Down?

Harris Creek

Up or Down?

Two Gator Creek

Up or Down?

Mud Creek

Up or Down?

This reflection was so vivid that it was somewhat disorienting to approach.

Bridge in town of Suwannee, where the river enters the Gulf of Mexico.

Special Encounters

Excerpt From Log, February 2001:

"As we were getting ready to leave Suwannee Gables, Old Town, an elderly couple (in their 70's yet) came ashore.

They are kayaking all of the Suwannee (210 miles) and will head down to the Gulf of Mexico tomorrow. They have a double kayak with all their gear and camp ashore."

A really loaded kayak for such a long trip... at least they were going down stream!

"Very Interesting couple. From Germany. First time in the States, but they kayak through Europe and New Zealand, too.

They said it was free to bring a kayak on the plane to New Zealand.

The woman said that they had never been in the U.S. before and the one thing that stood out as they came down the river was that in America the men did all the cooking outside."

Only 170 miles to go, "Auf Wiedersehen!"

They left before seeing the Captain cooking!

Excerpt From Log, March 1997:

Day 4

"Oklawaha to Silver Springs. Water clear to 20 feet as we approach Silver Springs.

Pull up in shady spot for lunch. One monkey appears, then another, then another. Had to pull away when they started to climb on boat for our lunch."

(We were told that they had escaped from a zoo and propagated, but since then we have heard differently.)

Quite a surprise...looking and seeing a monkey staring down at us!

Somebody actually brought them here...and they love it!

Excerpt From Log, May 2007:

Day 2

"Try to get on St. Mary's River at St. Mary's. River is tidal and to high to launch. Check out Scott's Landing just across Florida border. Too remote to leave car and trailer.

Back to St. Mary's. Tide is down somewhat. Get boat launched at 1:30 pm. Head up river. Stop at what looks like an island. Captain starts fire onshore to cook lamb chops. While cooking a friendly retriever shows up. Can't see any houses around, but dog has a collar with name "Shadow."

Shadow helps Captain cook. Even tastes a piece to make sure it's cooked."

"I think they're done!"

"When we leave, Shadow wants to come with us. Captain says Shadow told him he was an old sea-dog and if we let him come with us, he'd do all the cooking. Captain says we already have one of those. Shadow was very special."

"Please let me come with you. I'll do all the cooking."

"At least promise you'll come back."

Excerpt From Log, February 2002:

"Head south. Warmer this a.m. Clear sky, calm. Gas up at Holly Bluff. Buy manatee T-shirts.

Approach Blue Springs. See baby manatee tied to a buoy in the water. Nearby, a Manatee Research boat is loading it's mother onto the boat. Turns out she's sick and is being taken to Sea World for care. Quite a trick getting a 15 foot, 1000 pound manatee on a small boat. If that wasn't enough of a feat, they then loaded her onto a truck."

Baby manatee tied to a buoy.

Loading mother manatee onto a rescue boat.

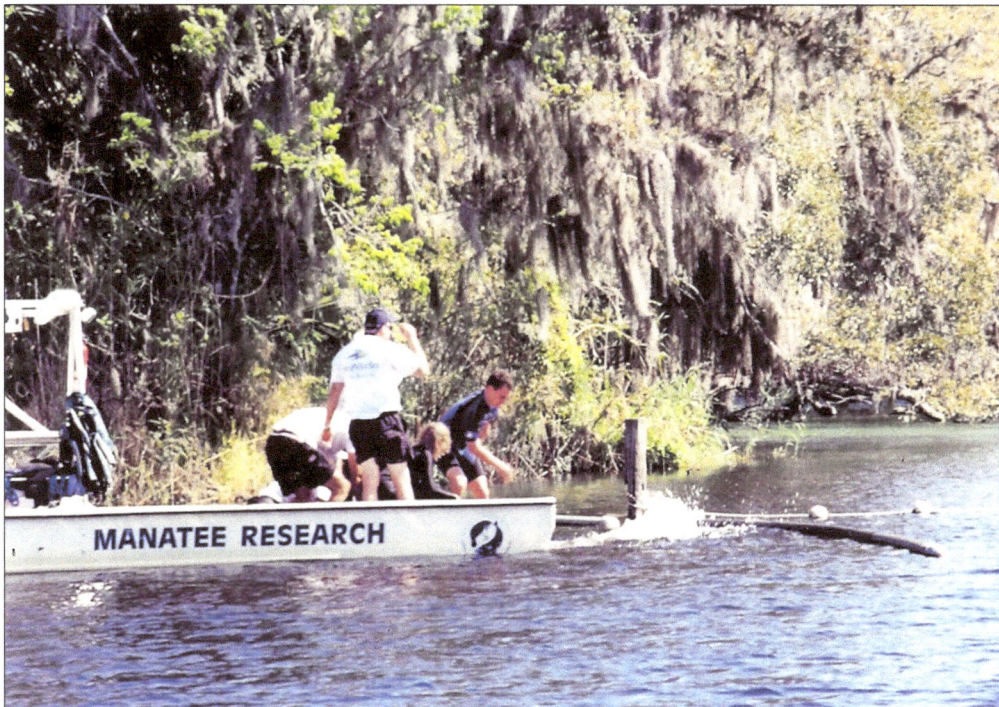

Throwing baby back into the spring.

"The baby manatee was released into Blue Springs where they said the other manatees would care for it."

Excerpt From Log, February 2007:

Day 2

"Head up Route 98 to Fort Basinger. Head south on 721. Find Butler Bluff. Launch and head north for about 20 minutes. Calm and warm. Water too shallow to continue. About face. Head south.

Cross main Kissimee River east into Old River Run. Connect with main river.

North to Butler Bluff Park. See four small dogs walking across grass.

Amazed to see the second "dog" is a baby raccoon. Incredible!"

"Hey look! Four small dogs out for a stroll."

"Wait a minute! That ain't no dog!"

A beautiful example of how we can all get along together if we really try!

Excerpt From Log, January 2009:

Day 1

"Cold morning. 38 degrees. Can't get up Harris Creek. Blocked by big trees and very low water. Motor just sucking up mud big time. It's raining hard now. Love the sound of the rain on the canvas.

Tie up in main river for lunch. Surrounded by gulls circling and diving for bread crumbs. In the tree overhead, vultures are huddled in pairs. Limpkin yells at us. Egrets and blue herons stand by watching. Fish are jumping. Tell limpkin to calm down. He does. Ibises snuggling together on ground to keep warm."

Day 2

"Still cold. Find a cut deep enough for lunch. Sun comes out. See a big gator. It's up on the bank. It looks dead. Kedger wants to get a real close photo...so we moved closer."

One of the biggest we've seen.

He lunged straight at the boat. Only alligator we've met with an attitude.
Guess he's entitled. After all, it is mating season!

72

Excerpt From Log, January 2001:

Day 4

"On Kissimee. Go through lock 5-65. Spot enormous gator. Two more on opposite bank. Another huge one. Gators everywhere. Water's low. Try to go on Old River Run, but too shallow. Head back north.

Captain spots a sheep on edge of bank. Wonder if he's stuck in the mud. We get close. Captain jumps in, but starts to disappear before our eyes! Mud is up to his thighs. We grab him and pull, pull, pull. He gets in the boat covered in mud."

Sheep stuck in mud at edge of plants.

"Try to pry sheep loose with paddles, but no luck. Seems to know we are trying to help."

Can't dig her out with a paddle.

"Back boat further down, where footing is more solid. Barb and Sandy walk gingerly toward sheep from shore. Start sinking in the mud. Dennis throws boat canvas over mud to stop us from sinking."

We spread out boat canvas, so First Mate and Kedger can crawl over mud to sheep.

"I hold Barb's pants– she wraps line under sheep's belly. We each take an end and pull, pull, pull. Sheep struggles– and helps– out she comes! Yea! Hooray! She's out. What a rescue! Think this is our calling."

(Wish we had photos of us crawling across mud to tie line around her belly. We were pretty busy and there were gators all around!)

She wobbles up to pasture, then looks back and baas, "Thank you!"

"Take boat out at Oasis.

Dinner at 'Ruby Tuesdays.'

Decide to call the sheep 'Lucky Ruby'."

A few more extraordinary sights we have come across...

An otter, who showed us the way out of Little Juniper Creek into Lake George.

An Armadillo browsing on Hontoon Island.

Not a "sea cow", but a cow marooned on a flooded Econolockahatchee. (native meaning: River of Mounds)

Some "friends" dropped by on the St. John's River.

At Cross Creek we came upon the historic home of Marjorie Kinnan Rawlings, the famous author of "the Yearling."

Water Levels

We're often asked, "Even though there are hundreds of miles of streams, don't you find yourselves repeating the same stretches over and over again?"

To some extent, yes. But, its never boring because Northern Florida has real seasons. We are there for fall, winter and spring; and the views can be quite different for each season. When the trees are bare, you can see further into the forest. When the water levels are lower, the banks are more exposed and you see more animal life.

Santa Fe River water marks.

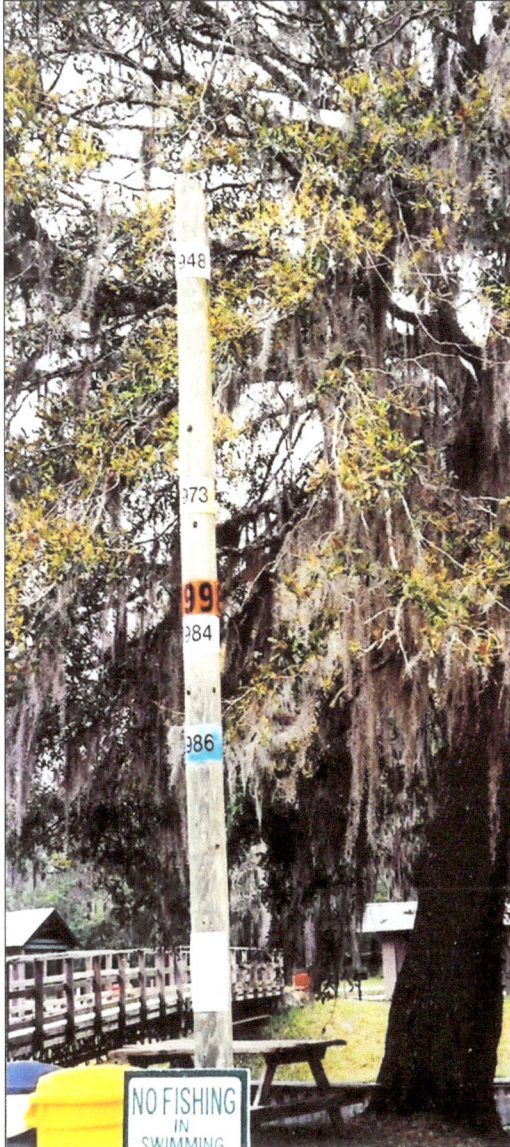

Water levels marked by year at Hart Springs on the Suwannee River in 2002.

Water levels have always fluctuated considerably from year to year, depending on the summer rain and the hurricane season. It is our feeling that the water levels have been getting lower over the last decade.

The large natural underground water storage areas, called aquifers, are not being replenished by sufficient rainfall, most of which runs off the land into the rivers and streams.

Increased population and increased industrial and agricultural development is putting increasing pressure on the need for water.

The St. John's Water Management District is one of five state management districts with the mission of ensuring water supply, water quality and flood protection.

Their mission is vital to Florida, and we wish them well.

Obstacles

An "Odyssey" is a long journey with obstacles.

These are typical of the expected obstacles we meet while traveling on the narrow creeks, some not much wider than "The Horny Owl."

A creek off the Suwannee River.

"Almost!"

"We're through!"

Creek blocked by aquatic plants...
first try to paddle through...

if that doesn't work... throw the grappling hook...

boat pulls the hook,
clears a channel...

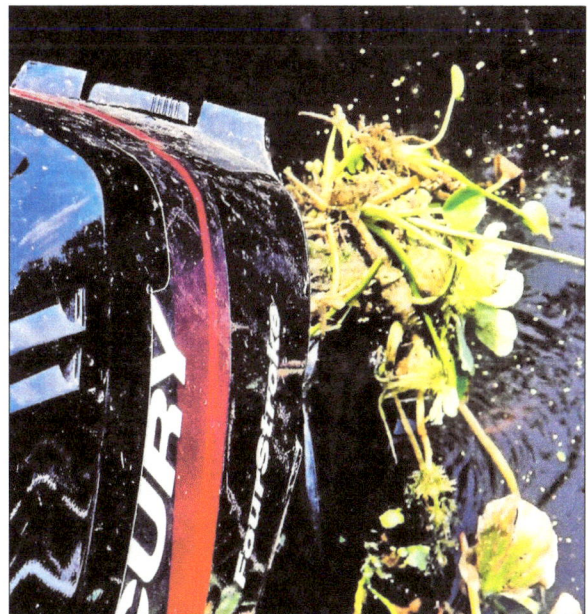

we clean the propeller...
and we're on our way!

Our "normal" trips involve getting caught in the weeds, overhanging branches, hitting submerged logs, etc. These are a few of the unexpected obstacles we have encountered.

Excerpt from log, January 2003

Day 2

"Head up Santa Fe. Water up several feet. Cold. Crisp and clear day. All bundled up. See broad winged hawk, muscovy ducks, whistling ducks. Black tupelo trees line the river (red leaves.)

Sun warms up as we cruise. Absolutely beautiful. End up at Ginnie Springs, a wonderfully maintained park. Picnic tables and grills everywhere. Cavern in the springs for scuba divers. Water about 70. Not a soul in the park; we have it to ourselves. (It's winter up here for Floridians.) Have lunch and head back down Santa Fe. About ten minutes later, we are headed into white water—moving fast with rocks."

Entering the rapids.

"Pontoons get hung up on the rocks. Push with boat hooks. Can't budge it. Current is taking us further on rocks. Battling rocks, current and branches. Try kedging– throw grappling hook out, catches on something but can't hang on. Lose the hook.

Captain gets in water. We all start jumping up and down. Boat gets off portion of the rock. Captain can't hold boat alone against current. Sandy gets in water and, "Together...one. two, three...push!" Boat swings around. Barb and Marie are guiding us around branches. All of a sudden we're free!"

"Dennis and Sandy have to get in boat as current takes it away. Sandy is in a hole...pulls herself up with everything she has. Dennis literally pole vaults over the stern railing.

We did it! We did it!"

First Mate trying to rock us off a rock...doesn't that look like Katharine Hepburn?

Excerpt from log, January 2007

Day 3

"Wake up to rain and spitting rain. Forecast is for clearing so decide to head out. Down to Mount Dora Canal across Lake Eustis. Cypress trees outstanding going through canal. Cross Lake Beauclaire to Lake Apopka Canal. Very shallow past buoys that warn us of extremely low water. Turn around back into Lake Beauclaire and hit very shallow water. Mud, mud, mud. Totally stuck.

Airboat passes us. They're too noisy. Don't like them."

"Poles just sink in mud. Try to paddle. We are stuck. Period.

After over two hours, hear the "now wonderful" sound of the airboat coming back. Sees us. Comes over across the mud. We put out a tow line and it tows us across the mud to deeper water.

The airboat is the only boat we saw that day, and is the only type of boat that could rescue us. We now believe in miracles.

Head for the ramp and home. Captain says being towed 20 feet behind an airboat would make a very good punishment for misdemeanors."

Excerpt from log, February 2005

Day 3

"Head for Lake Okeechobee. Stop short of lock for lunch. Thoroughly entertained by while pelicans swimming and diving in unison. Fantastic. Cruise slowly back.

Stop at Rivergate Park. Find ramp. Take boat out. Stop for gas on Route 1. Leaving gas station hit pothole. Something happened. Drive a few yards. Boat at an angle. Tires wobble and blow. Boat is almost sideways. Manage to pull off US 1 on large grassy area."

"Deputy Sheriff stops to help. Hosannah! Calls, trying to find towing truck large enough. Three hours later tow truck arrives and lifts trailer and boat on flat bed truck. A real feat as axle keeps sliding back. Takes it up motor first."

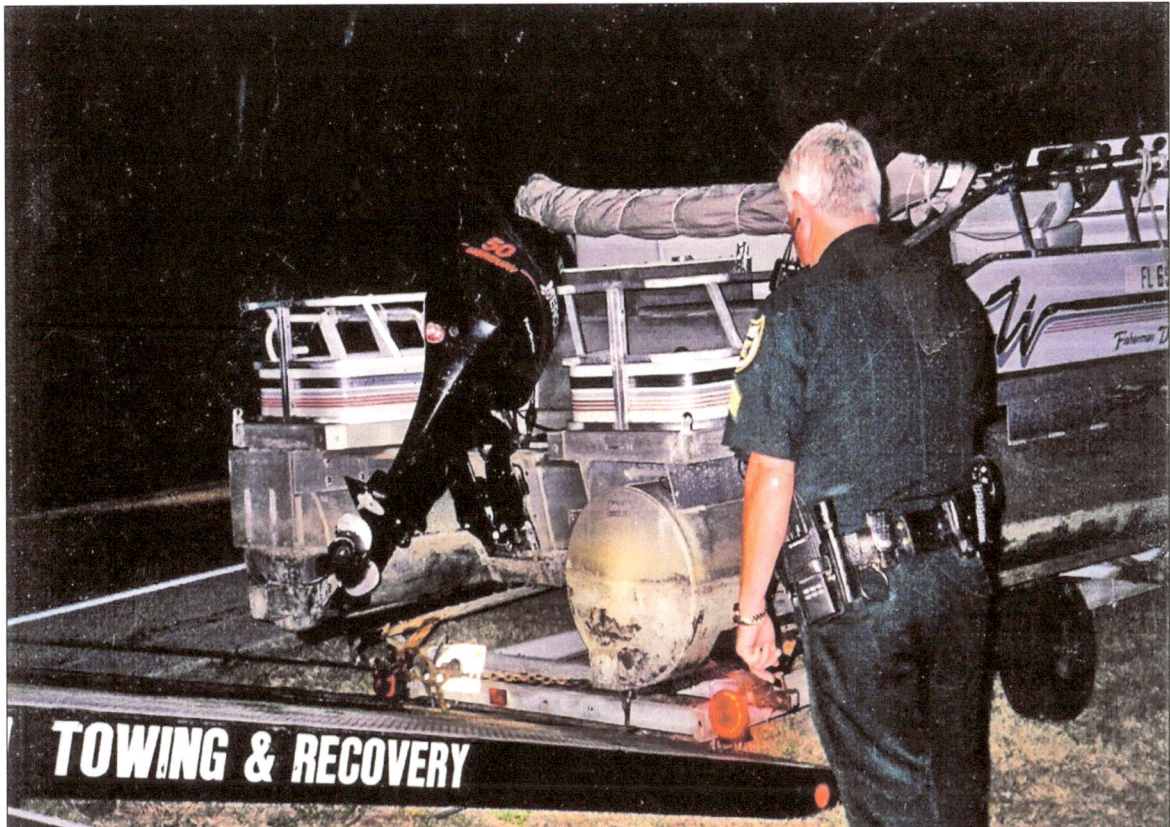

The Deputy Sheriff was really great.

"While waiting in dark, Sandy, Marie and Barb sat on edge of road. Men in trucks and cars kept on stopping to help women in distress. Captain says it's dangerous with trucks stopping in dark and suggests we stay back and he'll wait for police. He does, and first truck that comes by stops and asks if he needs help. It's a woman driver. Equality of the sexes has come a long way."

Excerpt from log, February 2009

Day 2

"See a cut we've never seen before. Marker 21. Get stuck pretty fast. Heavy log underneath and floating lumps of spatterdock roots. Finally get loose.

Come to a fork. Take various turns. After two hours, start to go back. Getting dark. Short of gas. Realize for the first time we are lost. Which turn did we come from? Turn around again on a different cut. Sheer luck! We end up where we came in, but from a different direction.

As a result of this, Captain intends to buy a 'GSP.'"

"That wasn't a typo!

We bought Green Spray Paint.

If we get lost in an unknown area and can't recognize which way we took, 'A little dab'll do ya!'"

Uncensored Answers to "Personal" Questions

"If on the boat ten hours a day, how, you know, er, where do you, er, you know what I mean?"

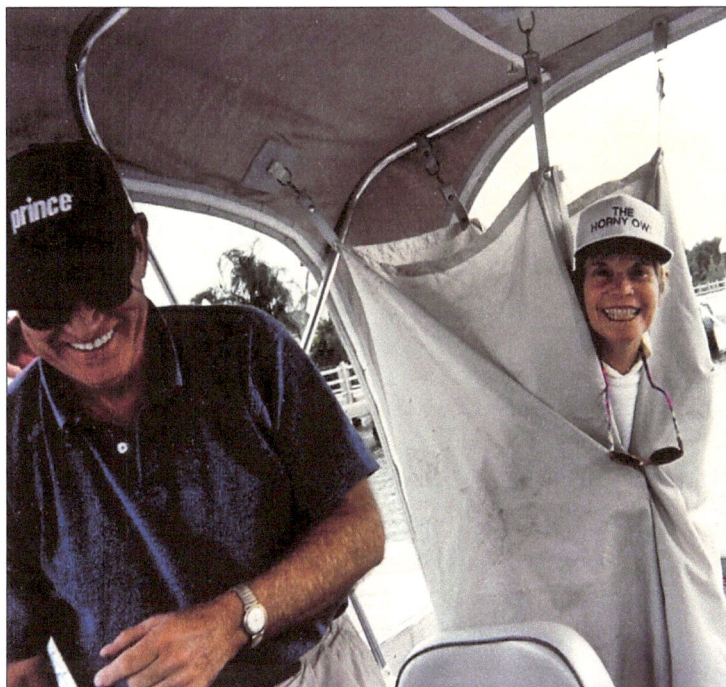

We are proud to share this one with the astronauts.

Actually we did start with a space age contraption...a porta potty inside a canvas tube, which zipped up from the bottom. (No pun intended.)

Unfortunately, when the sun was shining, it was almost transparent. Anyway, we couldn't use it for laughing!

So we went back to the old plastic bucket.

"What are the sleeping arrangements?"

We don't sleep on "The Horny Owl." These trips are for pleasure not penance. We always have single rooms and over the years have stayed in fish camps, like Bass Haven in Welaka and Blair's Jungle Den in Astor. If there is no fish camp, we can usually hitch a ride to a local motel.

Bass Haven in Welaka, now gone. (above) Blair's Jungle Den in Astor. (below)

"How do you handle the insects?"

We don't have to. We have never been bothered by insects on any of our trips. Maybe it's because our trips are between October and May and North Florida is a temperate climate, not sub-tropical like South Florida. It can get nippy sometimes in the South but downright freezing in the North. Maybe it's because we're on moving water.

There are, however, a group of creatures we look for on the very narrow cuts. They are spiders that string incredibly large webs between trees, some four or five feet across. They're called "golden silk orb spiders." Could be they're another reason why we haven't been bothered by insects.

Epilogue

After twenty years of incredible service, "The Horny Owl" went to pontoon heaven in 2012. It had encountered just too many obstacles, like submerged logs, and the pontoons were leaking badly. For a while, we tried draining them on slopes, but slopes are hard to find in Florida.

All is not lost, however! We now have a new pontoon boat. It is smaller in beam so presently we can now go on even narrower waters. There are still new waterways to explore and new wilderness to discover.

Name of the new boat? "The Horny Owl Too", of course!

As for the crew…they've had a few personal parts replaced, but are doing well. Now in our mid eighties, we are still tripping, and still singing the official Horny Owl Song:

"**How you gonna keep 'em down at Sea Oaks**
Now that they've seen Suwannee?
How you gonna keep 'em with the upscale folks
Now that they've been free?
How you gonna keep 'em on the tennis courts?
That ain't enough for me.
Suwannee, how I luv ya, how I luv ya,
That's where I want to bee eee eee!"

With sincere apologies to Stephen Foster, composer of the song, "Suwannee."

96

Acknowledgements

With thanks to:

Jean Hardcastle, for her continual review and patience.

Neighbors at Sea Oaks, for prompting the original "lecture."

Barbara Hanover, for her meticulous editing of the copy.

Brad Blanchard, for his proofing and encouragement in the very beginning.

Eunice Kelly, for her advice on distribution.

John Coughlin, for watching over The Horny Owl in the summer months.

Tom Conlin, of Aquamarine, Vero Beach, for keeping The Horny Owl purring quietly along.

Special thanks to:

Susie Evert, for being my publishing agent, and for the book's cover, copy layout and graphic design.
s.evert@sbcglobal.net

FLORIDA FOCUS
FEATURING: Sandy Lecklider, Marie Meckler, Barb Eccker and Dennis Hardcastle
TUESDAY, APRIL 20 ~ 5:00
COMMUNITY ROOM

For 16 years 3 women with 1 man have been traveling the streams, creeks and rivers of Florida's wilderness on a pontoon boat. They have made 89 four day trips so far.

PRESENTING
"THE ODYSSEY OF THE HORNY OWL"
...a pontoon boat with attitude

This program is an uncensored presentation of what really happens on the trips. No holds barred.

Wine and Cheese Reception Following
Speaker Buffet available at the Beach Club.

For dinner reservations call 234-4242.

DVDs available of this original "lecture." It's a Hoot!

please email s.evert@sbcglobal.net, subject line: Horny Owl DVD
(cost $10 plus postage)

Sandy Lecklider   Barb Eccker   Marie Mekler